ABOUT THIS BOOK

Whether you live in the town or the country, not a day passes without you seeing a variety of vehicles, be it on land, water or in the air. Indeed a lot of toys are vehicles themselves. Children have a great interest in things that go, because of their immense variety of movement, size, shape and colour.

Using this book to help, encourage your child to become observant and ask questions about the vehicles you see from your window or when you go out for a walk. Talk about how they move on a very simple level, such as, "Aeroplanes fly in the air. A boat floats on the water," and so on. Ask questions like, "Can you see any wheels on this machine? How do you think it moves along?" Compare sizes of vans and cars, and use this opportunity to introduce new words like large, huge, tiny, long, short, etc. Children will enjoy playing with toy versions of the vehicles they have seen outside or in this book and they will have fun looking through the book to find them. All of these things will add to their general knowledge, their early reading skills and enjoyment of learning.

Rhona Whiteford
(B.A. (Open), Cert. Ed., former Head of Infants)

James Fitzsimmons
(Cert. Ed., Head of Infants)

things that go

written by
Rhona Whiteford and
James Fitzsimmons

illustrated by Terry Burton

Filmset in Nelson Teaching Alphabet
by kind permission of
Thomas Nelson and Son Ltd.

Copyright © 1990 by World International Publishing Limited.
All rights reserved.
Published in Great Britain by World International Publishing Limited,
An Egmont Company, Egmont House, P.O. Box 111, Great Ducie Street,
Manchester M60 3BL.
Printed in DDR.
ISBN 0 7235 4114 0

A CIP catalogue record for this book is available from the British Library

cars and buses

Cars and buses carry people along the roads on journeys to different places.

Have you ever been on a bus?
Where did you go to?

lorries and vans

Lorries and vans carry workmen on their way to do jobs.
Some carry things from shops and factories.

How many of these different sorts of lorries and vans have you seen?

police vehicles

The police drive special cars, vans and motorbikes.
They have sirens and flashing blue lights on their vehicles to warn people that they are coming.

Have you ever heard a police car's siren?
Was it very loud?

fire engines

Firemen speed along the road in their fire engines to wherever there is a fire, so that they can put it out quickly.

A fire engine is large.
Do fire engines have flashing lights and sirens?

ambulances

Ambulance men and women care for people who are sick or hurt. They take them to hospital in an ambulance.

Have you seen an ambulance hurrying down the road with its lights flashing?

construction vehicles

Huge machines help to build our roads and houses.
They are very strong and noisy.

Which machines do you think can dig holes?

farm vehicles

The farmer has many big machines to help him on the farm.

Has a tractor got big or small wheels?

bicycles and toys

Toys that go are great fun, but they are only for riding at home, in the playground or on the pavement.

Older children can ride their bicycles on the road if they are careful. Can you ride a bike?

trains

Trains can go very fast, but they can only move on rails.
They take people or goods on long journeys.

Do trains have wheels?

boats and other watercraft

Boats can move on water but not on land.
The wind makes some boats move.
Others have motors to make them go.

Can you see a submarine?
It moves underneath the water.

aeroplanes

Aeroplanes fly through the air.
They go very fast indeed on long
journeys across land and sea.

Aeroplanes have wings to help them fly.
Which animal has wings?

spacecraft

Some machines can fly right away from the earth into space.

Would you like to go in a spacecraft?